LOCAL
EXTINCTIONS

LOCAL EXTINCTIONS

a book of poems by
MARY QUADE

Gold Wake

For my family
and the animals who watch over us all—
past, present, future.

Contents

// 1

Birthday Party Magician - 5
Mole - 6
Egg - 7
Daffodils - 8
Magic Fingers - 9
Cow Puppet - 10
Wealth - 11
How to Use a Single-Lens Reflex - 13
Love Poem with Bodies - 14
Gull - 16
Workbench - 17
From Old Doctor Carlin's Receipt Book
and Household Physician - 18

// 2

Historical Marker, Rest Stop, Jackson County, Wisconsin - 25
Killing Songbirds the Compassionate Way - 27
To Bear - 29
Phobia Poems - 30
Rickey Henderson Breaks the Record for Stolen Bases
in a Season, Milwaukee, 1982 - 33
Two Exercises in Stopping Time - 35
Bluing - 37
The Middle School Cheerleader - 38
In the Toy Hall of Fame - 40
Amish Boy with Remote Control Car - 43
Amish Boy Gesturing at the Road - 44
Adjusting the Depth of Field - 46
Stinging Things - 47

// 3

The Sacrifice - 51
The Fig - 53
Homage to Small Hurts - 55
Framing the Shot - 57
Historical Marker Partially Obscured by Shrubs - 58
Loneliness as a Tour of Covered Bridges,
Ashtabula County, Ohio - 59
Sky Dive - 62
Skyway Drive-In Theater, Madison, Ohio - 64
Missing - 65
Measuring Exposure - 67
Clothesline - 69
First Place at the County Fair - 70

LOCAL EXTINCTIONS

1

I cannot describe to you the extreme beauty of their aerial evolutions when a Hawk chanced to press upon the rear of a flock. At once, like a torrent, and with a noise like thunder, they rushed into a compact mass, pressing upon each other towards the center. In these almost solid masses they darted forward in undulating and angular lines, descended and swept close over the earth with inconceivable velocity, mounted perpendicularly so as to resemble a vast column and, when high, were seen wheeling and twisting within their continued lines, which then resembled the coils of a gigantic serpent.

//

It may not perhaps be out of place to attempt an estimate of the number of Pigeons contained in one of those mighty flocks and of the quantity of food daily consumed by its members. The inquiry will tend to shew the astonishing bounty of the great Author of Nature in providing for the wants of his creatures.

John James Audubon
on the passenger pigeon, *Ectopistes migratorious*

BIRTHDAY PARTY MAGICIAN

The trick depends on subtlety and suddenness,
a year turning into the next, the universe
expanding—the illusion, not change, but things
staying the same.
                    Inside his black jacket,
his body lingers, as if off stage, a dressing room
for colored squares, ropes, the harnessed dove. At what
age will we begin to disbelieve, will we leave
our silk hat, vaguely aware?
                              Inside his sleeve, a renaissance;
a device, brutally simple, keeps the dove in place, waiting
for his hand, the feint of flame obscuring
wings' release. The rabbit abides inside its chamber.
                                                    He pulls
an endless silent ribbon from his mouth,
a white confession: *The wand
is just a kind of stick.*
                          But we have given up
our dexterous guessing. Our ears tire
of bearing coins. We are balloons, penetrated by pins,
unpopped.
          Perfidious thin air
out of which it all appears—
                          we want
our boxes opening to nice gifts. We want
our cake—the moment when he takes the jacket off,
the lining flecked with feathers, droppings—and
turns himself into a man.

MOLE

A dark thing grows under the bright, insinuating.
The lawn, blemished with soft eruptions,
loose mounds. I find one dying
beneath the rose bush and then
it is dead and I can
hold it, this secret.
Nose, still supple. Its tined fin-like forelegs
for diving, surfacing—land's
inconsiderable whale.
I probe fur for eyes. On its side,
several pierces—wounds. Why
would it leave the ground,
blow a perfect cover? In every operation,
someone is working the inside,
with a one-syllable name, a gray suit,
a refined blindness.
Imposture—
a small kind of cancer.
All so-called solids are perforated;
something can always get in,
combine, bond. My theory
that I could stand here
without sinking
seems to be unfounded. A tunnel
erodes the ground's integrity
while maintaining, even bolstering,
its own. The only evidence
in any mystery is a tiny,
but perceptible, hole.

EGG

The perplexity of the egg—
both sturdy and designed to break;
a chicken conjured this,
fluffed in her nest box, vexed
by her bird urge to sit, by her
disturbing burdens—the eggs
inside the cage of her bones
eternally emerging, one by one,
like the same hot thought.
                              Out in the yard,
euphoric hens,
disabused of duty,
grab at scratch, dig baths of dirt,
hunt the inscrutable bug.
I put the egg in my jacket pocket
where I find it later, ticking.
                              Each egg
forms, fittingly, in layers—
a cipher of shell and white and air
around the unscrambled yolk.
I turn up the heat, crack it
into the pan, add salt.

The code
of husbandry says this:
take the egg,
her beak reaching for your hand;
protect her from her brooding,
from her tendency to believe
something dear will come
of what she divulges
while alone in the clucking dark.

DAFFODILS

An emanation—the yellow by the road,
each flower, an announcement. No one
could plan this show. Even my own
swaths shock me—
is this what I meant,
what I buried in the fall with my trowel,
that stout accomplice? Somehow,
clumps appear in unmown fields,
by isolated stumps in plain woods—
shadows of intentions.
Even beside a Chicago expressway,
among the sheddings of cars,
the burned-out flares, I saw
their petaled horns blowing—
all debris of accident.
Narcissus didn't mean
to look into the pool—
to be broken by such beauty.
Sometimes, there is no choice.
Along the house, beaten down by rain,
muddied blooms—I cut
and wash; it seems a shame
not to listen—though the bud, delicate,
is only voice. The source,
poisonous and hard, hides deep below.

MAGIC FINGERS

It quickly carries you into the land of 'tingling
relaxation and ease.' Try it—you'll feel great.

Manmade earthquake in remote motels
off state routes—motorized mattress,
metal box on the nightstand with a slot
for quarters, for fifteen minutes of rattle. Late,
the pool closed, but there dozed
this pleasure and we awoke it, fed it
change. The same coin at the petting
zoo bought us a handful of chow
which turned the braying ass into teeth
gently nipping our palms so we could stroke
a dusty neck and pose. Do you see
any difference? The bedspread metamorphosed.
The ceiling stains blurred. Nothing impure, instead
just vacancy. The road dead until we rose.

Cow Puppet

The illusion of voice, my mute hand moving your mouth
as I utter what I assume you would—*moo,*
moooo—smooth ululation of cow.
I feel the confused kinesthesia of myself as you.
What might you choose, if you could? Bones,
maybe. A throat, to speak and swallow. A brain.
An escape from my wrist. Or is this my own
wish list? No, I say nothing to gain
by truly being what you resemble, or by the blur
of sentience, dilemma's pain, regret. Puppet,
relieve me for a moment of some words and gestures.
My fingers warm your fuzz. My thumb, a jaw, chews. Let
me ruminate as cow, grass-numb, glass eyes wide,
and see myself at arm's length, and not try to get inside.

WEALTH

Summer:
plane descending under clouds, below the wings
emerge fans of sandy soil and
speckles of sapphire—
baseball diamonds and above-ground pools—
this land's handprints of hardworking
princes.
            My childhood aqua envy—
how I craved tasting the neighbors' blue
splash and bleachy haze, their tidy
waves, lawns beglamoured with
marigolds. To step outside the sliding door
and float—a petal in a bowl,
ice in an enchanted glass. All riches
seemed to me some version of
a dish of sparkle.
                        I've now felt places
hotter than the heart
of this country, poor tropical spots unpopulated
by pools—what would they give
for such water?
                    And now, too, I notice
how in these backyard crowns
no one ever swims. A pump
hums an inflated raft around the surface,
a disinterested whirl. A ball skims
the margins, ripples along the rim—
I wish, I wish, I wish.
                        Gazing out the kitchen window
past the glinting ring,
a woman dreams of paradise, of the Milky Way
dripping around her wrists. In the sink, she rinses

a cabbage and dreams of
clasping the sun.

How to Use a Single-Lens Reflex

The camera, slumberless, cannot shut out
its visions. Even resting in your palm,
lens cap on, it beholds the numb black.
Without you, it forgets—all
oblivion. You are the mnemonic,
the trick of recall.
            The body
is a dark hallway the mind
winds through. A door briefly blinks, and the film,
enlightened, moves on in darkness.
                   I notice the invisible
worries you. You want
to pop the body open, study
flesh as ghost.
      See,
you can't. The darkness carries
                without gestation.
What you saw stays what you saw,
and, like any dream, is damaged
by brilliant awakening.

Love Poem with Bodies

We share bodies,
carnal and
carcass,
to have and to hold.
Remember the caress of
the crescent of rabbit
caught mid-leap in the garden fence, frozen,
the puffs of fur, the paws that had once
encoded the snow—*dash, dot, dot.*
You unscrambled it from wire.
Or the woodcock you brought me, a present
found in a parking lot, eyes fastened open,
needle beak keen in my palm.
Together we negotiated the toad,
bloated with sun, legs
thrust out—unburst,
nervous as a mine.
I have waited, watching the window,
for your truck to come home,
for you to bury the poor duck
I separated from road, broken
into components of webbing, wing, and bill.

So many bodies to minister to,
to divine. Only the dead let us
see their bones. But don't we know
at least our own insides, and each, the other's?
Like the summer afternoon
we set our wine glasses down, let go
of their stems, to tend to
an ill raccoon stirring in the barn.
You didn't have to tell me,

as you pinned its neck with a pitchfork,
to take the shovel, deliver the blow.

GULL

If I knew anything about seagulls,
I could translate their flapping beyond
white against sky or waves.
I'm certain they aren't all the same
bird, probably not even close
friends. Herds of flocks floating—
message-less bottles. They've flown so far only
to have me not wonder. I gloat
about the great blue heron gracing my gaze,
the bald eagle balancing on breeze
above the bluffs. These, too, might seem dull
in numbers. Out on Erie, a gull lifts,
sleek and anonymous, unjealous
of the scenery, which would languish
without it. I promise to learn more—a vow
I know will vanish into all the other vows.

WORKBENCH

After a man dies,
his wife descends someday
to the basement
to find the cure
for the door wailing on its hinges,
always sticking somewhere
between open and closed.
And there on the well-pounded workbench,
the WD-40—blue and yellow can, nozzled:
Lubricates, Protects, Penetrates—
its sweet, oily odor
like it's worked hard all afternoon
and needs a beer.
                    And there, too,
under the bug-crumbed shop light,
the vise, reliable,
with its unrelenting grasp; the lidless
jelly jars itchy with screws;
the giddy level,
its trapped bubbles;
and the crowd of small
broken things
maybe not worth fixing.

From Old Doctor Carlin's Receipt Book and Household Physician

> *Parsley—Something Worth Knowing. If after having bruised some sprigs of parsley in the hands, one attempts to rinse glasses, they will suddenly snap or break.*
>
> —Dr. Carlin

ACCIDENTS

Drowning Person, To Restore

Carry the body with the head slightly raised—
a reminder that life requires pride—then
remove all clothing and rub skin with a warm
brick and dry worsted socks. The world is sick
to death of succumbing, of sinking into the sea.
Raise the arms—the lungs fill, imitating breath.
Do not give up effort for twelve hours. Do not
allow crowding. Do not hang
the body by its feet. Do not, under any circumstances,
put it into a bath.

Limbs, Frozen

Determine the difference between ice and
hesitation, then select the method
of thaw. All pauses demand
immediate attention. Otherwise
one is always waiting around for spring.

Oysters, Over-Eating of

Like stumbling on an uneven path, it comes upon
one suddenly. The oyster never loses its surprise—
the cold brine-startled morsel on its
astonished shell. It's a wonder to find
one could have one's fill. Trust me,
one can't. Wait a few moments for the chill to pass.
Have another. Imagine inside one's belly
the uncultured pearl.

FOR FARMERS

Remedy for Wind

Cows are most susceptible;
they refuse, unlike horses, to give in,
to fly. They suffer the sky
changing, the grass lashing their legs. One cannot
rid them of their unwinged obstinacy.
Never use dogs or stones, but encourage
the herd toward shelter—a hedge or cordial barn—
or risk having them fall, like rain.

Bird Skins, To Cure

An amateur may not be successful at first,
since these, like hiccoughs, can be difficult
to cure. Treat the skin
tenderly, stroking in the direction of feathers, until
the skin is still. When completed, one will behold
a perfect specimen, artfully mounted,
indistinguishable from the living thing.

Cats Catching Chickens, To Cure

Tie one of the chickens around the cat's neck
and make her wear it three days. Exercise
firmness; guilt is a limp hen dangling,
weighing down one's pounce.

GENERAL HOUSEHOLD

Life Preserver, A Very Simple

If a person falls into water, a common
felt hat can be placed upon the surface,
rim down and bear a man up for hours.
But if one can't fathom floating, instead
take care to keep one's balance by
never lifting one's feet, and avoid
all water that won't be contained in a glass.

The Art of Shaving, Made Easy

The razor is only a very fine
saw and one must clear the beard
to find the scape of the face.
Warm the blade next to one's heart.
Start near the lip and slip toward the
throat. This is not the time
to think of her illegible lashes, of the
semiology of her hand not hiding
an insuppressible yawn.

Old Blood Stains, To Dissolve

Unlike broth and wine, blood necessarily

remains indelible, and one may regret
one's frantic scrubbing. Better to
disguise it among like blotches, or adopt
a habit of fatigue, of replying resignedly,
"Oh *that*," while waiting for something to
break that one can easily mend.

2

Here again the tyrant of the creation, man, interferes, disturbing the harmony of this peaceful scene. As the young birds grow up, their enemies, armed with axes, reach the spot to seize and destroy all they can. The trees are felled and made to fall in such a way that the cutting of one causes the overthrow of another or shakes the neighboring trees so much that the young Pigeons, or *squabs*, as they are named, are violently hurried to the ground. In this manner also, immense quantities are destroyed.

//

The Pigeons were still passing in undiminished numbers and continued to do so for three days in succession. The people were all in arms. The banks of the Ohio were crowded with men and boys incessantly shooting at the pilgrims, which there flew lower as they passed the river. Multitudes were thus destroyed. For a week or more, the population fed on no other flesh than that of Pigeons, and talked of nothing but Pigeons.

John James Audubon

HISTORICAL MARKER, REST STOP, JACKSON COUNTY, WISCONSIN

*The largest nesting on record anywhere occurred in this
area in 1871. The nesting ground covered 850 square
miles with an estimated 136,000,000 pigeons.*
     —inscription on marker

In Audubon's painting, the birds court—she leans over
her perch to thrust her bill into his below,
his throat arched, wings flared. The rest
is spare—two branches, some moss; the pair alone,
somehow, despite the flock of millions.
                                        I pause
in my wandering, if miles murmuring by on a band of highway
can be wandering, with the curve of road catching
curve of road. You, home,
states away. Between traffic and toilet, I read about
the feast of nests, birds hatching into
a land of traps and clubs and guns.
                                        Audubon and his Lucy
sail to Liverpool with 350 live passenger pigeons, gifts
bought for pennies each in a New York market.
The several years before, they'd spent
on separate continents, their letters migrating
over ocean—his, birds;
hers, worry—both brushed with love.
Before they reunited, her hair turned gray.
Her teeth, gone.
                                        Two other nearby markers
memorialize a fire and war. Of course,
all history is loss. Some things
even imagination's firmament can't hold.
                                        The painted birds
were dead; the living never still enough.

He himself shot them and before their bodies stiffened
pierced them with wire mounted on a board,
posed as in life, or almost, anyway—swift shifting
from mortal to immortal—a salvation.
                                    In this state
where I was raised, I feel displaced, a ghost
of me—residue in the present. I'm not sure what
I've left behind, or even what to take, so I pass by,
preserved by the illusion of traveling.
                                    In woods where
pigeons roosted, the ground lay snowed with
droppings, the tree limbs shattered
by a hurricane of birds—their weight, too much. Then,
having fed on what they needed,
any birds unmassacred moved on.

Killing Songbirds
the Compassionate Way

First, imagine
that you can save them
from their broken wings,
worm-filled wounds,
churned brains (for they are
determined as walnuts
to fall).
      Imagine
when you bring them into your house,
the ring of your thumb and forefinger
steadying their heads,
                  that the eye dropper
of sugared water
you slip inside their beaks
doesn't drown them (though
bubbles click
on their tongues);
             that their bones
are merely crumpled—
the weightlessness of paper—
and can be straightened out,
folded back in shape;
              that because they eat
the seeds and hop
across the cardboard box, squeaking,
they are only weak
or cold or stunned.
             (You will notice
when you find one, lapsed into
stillness on the ground, you
mistake their legs for twigs.)

Imagine, as the birds
percuss against the windows,
drop,
      that they saw you within—
your lids nictating,
your plumage unpreened—
and tried, suicidal,
to revive you,
to keep you
(suffering) alive.

To Bear

The polar bear is threatened—
on a list of things you shouldn't
stuff into your suitcase
and carry across a border.
The polar bear is threatening
to melt, like tissue, into the sea.
You can't capture
with infrared film a well-fed bear, its
fire hidden by fat and fur;
only hot breath appears,
bearless, an untranslated
warning. The polar bear
treads around the ice, sniffs for holes
where seals pop up for air, snaps
its jaws. There's a photo
of a man's head with scalp stripped off,
skull raw and spared.
A walrus is twice the size, but
this means nothing to me. What do trees
missed by lightning know? I know
only the bear in the small zoo,
chaos or cosmos of concrete,
always the pole of day
opposite the pole of night.
A window opens to the pool,
where the bear turns metronomical laps,
paw pushing off near my face,
again and again the thud on glass,
each hair hollow and clear,
though everyone sees
a bear white as a towel
thrown in.

PHOBIA POEMS

Fear of the Telephone

Was it ever cheerful, that sound they call
ringing? More an alarm—I answer it
and am startled into blindness. I can't find
the words to share with the air, faceless—
my *ums* fumbling alone along the line,
without my body, its silent excuses. And I suspect
the privacy of handsets, of transmitter and receiver.
Unempathetic emptiness, this room—
I want a witness
to what is told to me,
to what exactly is being asked.

Fear of Choking

It's not me—I know what I can swallow—
it's you, with your hard candy,
running around, breathing, as though breath were
sanctified—no; it may require saving.
And I'm unpracticed in such maneuvers
as you might need—in the sequences of
squeeze and pound, pinch and plead.
I like to think my feeble training would kick in,
but why should it? The world turns
bluer each day. Please take everything in small
bites. I can't even save myself.

Fear of Neighbors

With beds, with televisions, with drapes
or no drapes, with cigarettes and lighter fluid,
with machines that blow and chew, with babies inexplicably
growing, with lawns of scolded children,
with restraining orders, with my misdelivered mail,
with security lights trained on my
pillow, my closed eyes, with polite overtures
tossed across my untrimmed hedge,
landing like cats among my birds—Oh neighbor,
take this cup of sugar—my only sweetness—
and go; I never wanted to be close.

Fear of Being Abandoned in a Shopping Mall

You could decide to leave me anywhere
but here—and I would find my way
to forgiveness. But when I lose your face
to the flock of mannequins—their fashioned
familiarity—I feel desperate as mirrors.
Look around—things keep changing, and I'm sure
I've fallen behind and won't catch up—
the chorus line of hosiery legs kicking,
the enfilade of fragrances. You have lost, somewhere,
your patience, hard as a pocketbook. I will
materialize at some point, like I always do.

Fear of Turning into Salt

It won't be through turning back,
that much is clear; it will be through tears
melting the icy whatever else of me
and what I touch will dry up,

and they will call this preservation,
a way to save the meat. Or they will
scatter me on winter roads
and prevent all kinds of accidents.

Fear of Trees Falling

I worry this might happen, the world will listen
to the fulminous wind, and I'll step outside to find it,
bewildered with branches, broken. They have been standing
so long—they forget why. I
could give up this way, collapse, cold—
soft as shame. Such trusting,
to walk through the woods,
our spines seemingly solid enough. I see today a limb
has landed on the lawn—shade makes
a clumsy symbol, unsubtle foreshadowing. I know
about climaxes, about many forms of falling.

Fear of Finding a Body in the Forest

It's almost happened to us all—unaware,
we miss the bones among the needles. There was
the boy in the shallow grave, the rusted frame of his
bicycle. Or the despondent hiker
and his unlucky dog. Just off the path, a body awaits
my stumbling. The living are enough for me—
the way they're always turning up. Nothing is truly
missing. Last week a man confessed
to burying dozens of women he'd killed—
he'd lost track; he'd lost his reason
for letting them lie. Such motives—and yet, I'm afraid,
he was unmoved.

Rickey Henderson Breaks the Record for Stolen Bases in a Season, Milwaukee, 1982

I was there. I know it's true,
but memory starts someplace, then steps away and
runs for it. Over the details falls doubt—
that tarp covering the field's blades.
                                        I'm ten,
my first real game. Arriving in the stands, fans
find numbered seats. And when we leave,
I get a pennant. But in between?
A zero-pocked chart.
                          I remember
the A's Rickey Henderson on base. The dance of leading off,
pitcher turning, back and forth. He throws to first, plays
his role, and we play ours—traitors, wanting to catch history;
we boo our own. I don't remember this.
                                 I don't remember
wanting anything except home runs, so the man
up at the giant beer barrel can ride his chute
into the giant mug; the suds—released balloons. But
the wrong team's at bat. Perhaps I want
a sausage wrapped in foil. Or maybe all the sausages
since then have placed that sausage in my mind.
I know I didn't want what I couldn't have
expected, this blurred anecdote to share now over
beer and talk of baseball.
                        And what does
Henderson remember? Not me, a speck of kid near first,
about to watch him speed away. He remembers
a game just days before on his home field,
second base beckoning. The crowd awaits his gift. But

when he dives, the umpire calls him out. He'll tell
that bitter story for years.
                            The pitcher
tires of looking back; he must propel
the inning somewhere—
                            and then
Henderson is stealing—a few strides, a plunge—
I like this, like skipping a grade—
and the game stops. A ceremony, a man gives him
the base, stolen, yet earned. I know this.
                            I know this
is what is done. The robbed diamond, the base
alien in his grip, irrelevant—like what follows. Or maybe
what follows matters most. Despite the spectacle,
my team wins.
            And Henderson keeps stealing, stealing—
one moment in one place, and in the next, transported,
not like recollection, that stumbling, but instead,
impatient prophecy, a thing known with certainty
because it hasn't happened yet.

Two Exercises in Stopping Time

The Blur

A bird's wings lacy around
its still breast; a hand
     fanning the air
into a phantasm of fingers—
       tremors
in an anesthetized scene.
       You can see
the heart beat through the ribs.
Keep your eye open long enough.
       You can
see what lingers, wavering,
when the rest is dead.

The Instant

A ball, a leaf, a man
     suspended,
legs cocked
    against the shock of his
fall—
   these rudimentary suicides.

The ground wants everything back—
each dancer alighting on the stage.
       Here,
we have no satellites
      orbiting.
When you see matter lucid in flight—
the sharp crease of his strained brow—

you know, even on its way up,
it is on its way down.

BLUING

The dog was bad and mostly white and ran away
with the frequency of instinct—
                              that pulse—
her prurient fur in search of
carcasses—a fallen bird, a putrid
coon—or simply some manure, its effluent
perfume.
          So she'd slip from the yard
like light—slow, pooling,
unnoticeably gone,
                    only a white spot
for us to chase after, tearfully calling—our futile spell
against our fault of losing her,
our negligent leashes.
                      Then, hours later, her return—
neither furtive nor triumphant—just
a reappearance, an unrarefied
rankness about her, a filth-rubbed coat.

And we, apparently forgiven,
would coo her name, make promises,
as we carried her to the basement sink
for shampoo
            and bluing—the arcanum
for soiled shirts and dogs—
the trick of making a thing seem
bright by adding
a little blue.

THE MIDDLE SCHOOL CHEERLEADER

She vacillates between losing
and an unpredicted win. In the living
room, in front of the picture window at night,
its murky mirror,
she runs through the choreography
of cheer, the path of satellite
around some sun.
                        From outside,
she seems to mime the workings
of a particularly impenetrable
machine—the circulation of arms,
knee cranks, hands stamping the air
into discreet, clattering parts.
                        She mouths
Go, Go, Go—a plea.
                        Afternoons, she
launches across the lawn
in flaccid roundoffs, legs
never quite gathering
the elastic snap.
                        She's here
because she couldn't possibly
catch the ball herself, feed it
to the carnivorous goal. It stays
too much alive in her clutch,
flees.
        So she lifts one girl
to another girl's shoulders. Her sweater
hugs nothing, her skirt
flirts chastely
with her thighs.
                        In high school,

she won't make the squad—with their tease
of flips, their victory of firm
towers, their incommunicable
congenital pep, their splitting
themselves in two.

In the Toy Hall of Fame

Lincoln Logs

Easy to make a window—
logs locking into logs, points
in a debate—through which I see
the land large with states.
Hard to build a three-car garage.

Slinky

Hiccup of wire humping down
stairs sometimes, and sometimes
giving into tension halfway, a humming
tube, no momentum. I know how you feel, leaning
over a line. You smell like work.

Marbles

All I grasp is you can lose
your marbles, as clearly many have. I find them
scattered in the gravel drive, the flower bed, the
basement corners. Not aggies or cat's-eyes, just everyday
blues and whites, disguised as stones, not on a
roll. Dropped—small
memories—from use.

Mr. Potato Head

Dug from the dark garden of

someone's nightmare. I understand
eyes, but why the predator's smile,
the ears to hear me with?
I de-face you, leave only holes.

Frisbee

Curse you, identified flung object
my dog won't fetch.

Erector Set

Follow steps out of the commotion
of screws and plates and pulleys to erect
a windmill, or, better, a robot who moves
through mechanical mysteries and a motor
wired to double-D batteries that automatically
wear down, leaving creation
suspended, parts rusting, fusing
because I can't bear to dis-man-tle
something that behaves just like me.

Etch-A-Sketch

What does it mean to turn a knob?
Behind a veil of dust
something obeys.

Easy Bake Oven

For girls whose mothers don't trust them with real heat.
I don't want one, prefer stovetop,

the spark on gas, the troubled pot boiling.
Love anything I can stir.

Cardboard Box

I'm inside, the cushion of corrugation smothering
sound. If I'm a refrigerator,
I stay cool and numb. No one's allowed in unless
they know the password. Not that there's
room. Not that anyone has asked. Not that anyone
is looking for me, or ever will.

Stick

Sword, rifle, spear, wand—instruments of swift
indifferent change. After strong storms,
I step outside and the world beneath me
snaps with fun.

Amish Boy
with Remote Control Car

His back to me, woolen legs
moving down the gravel shoulder,
the boy shuffles, following something small in the road—
maybe a puppy
or a runaway ball. It's turning towards
spring around here, the vegetable gardens sprout
mounds of manure. The boy tails
this small thing. It's not getting away, it's not
veering into the pasture, bouncing further and further
among the wads of sheep. No, he'll catch it
sooner or later. But as I gain on him, I see what it is—
a steroidal jeep, miniaturized,
donut-sized wheels, wire antenna flicking
as he grips the control box. He steers it straight,
no 360s, no wheelies, no off-roading
in the grass flecked with litter,
just a steady cruise along the white line,
his plain concentration.
The irony isn't lost; it follows the path of the road.
If I weren't driving, I'd like to go for a walk.
If I weren't working, I'd like to shovel manure.
I'd like to grab a sheep and sink my hand in fleece,
touch hot skin.
The boy and I will each reach where we're going. And when I
arrive, I'll flip a switch, set the meter spinning. And later,
could I make it stop?
There are lots of dos and don'ts to both our ways.
I'm never clear on his,
but I know mine. Do not speed. Pass with care.
Thou shalt not covet thy neighbor's life.

AMISH BOY GESTURING AT THE ROAD

Where is the boy who looks after the sheep?

He's pumping
his fist
vigorously, elbow working it
up and down
in front of his body,
tight with clothes—

an obscene gesture!
How? I gasp. Behind him
turquoise and pink dresses shimmy
on the line. They look cotton,
but they're polyester. They feel
like motel sheets, I think,
never wearing out. Some have no
buttons to fall off,
only pins
biting the placket.
These people seem very practical
and impractical—
with their linoleum-floored bedrooms
and oil lamps burning
near white curtains always perfectly
open or perfectly closed.
Shouldn't the boy be using
this energy
to milk a cow or something?
His straw hat begins to slip.
A horse takes a step;
the blade slices through earth.
The boy's elbow
never wears out.

Oh. I see
what he wants. He wants
a passing semi-truck
to blow,
blow the horn.

ADJUSTING THE DEPTH OF FIELD

(after a version of Dorothea Lange's Migrant Mother,
Nipomo, California, March 1936*)*

The smaller the window
                    the more you will see
clearly—
          and the more you see clearly—
such focus—
              the more the world seems flat.

Decide what you would rather leave
nebulous, what you should hide
in the fog of its own shape:

                        the bleary
suitcase set with the suggestion of
                              an empty plate

              before the infant—less vague—

fading into his mother—
                    the crisp lines of her face—

the distinct pole holding up the lean-to,

                              the land beyond—
an impression of dust and trees.

                    We see

no ruined field—
              the tiny peas lost to frost—
no hint of work.

Stinging Things

after shootings in a Cleveland public high school

You were pruning the crabapple—
its branches choked with suckers
and callous sour fruit—
when something stung you on the ear,
as if to say to its pliant softness,
Now hear this,
the burn growing like hot gossip.

Then you saw the nest hanging above,
a child's head, wrapped in bandages,
disembodied, and the warnings
brimming from the mouth,
a tantrum of glassy wings.
Inside, chambers and chambers of flightless
angers—substance, but not yet shape.

3

September 1, 1914: The last passenger pigeon dies at the Cincinnati Zoo, Ohio.

//

And I saw an angel standing in the sun, who cried in a loud voice to all the birds flying in midair, "Come, gather together for the great supper of God, so that you may eat the flesh of kings, generals, and mighty men, of horses and their riders, and the flesh of all people, free and slave, small and great."

Revelation 19:17-18

THE SACRIFICE

...The god who answers by fire—he is God.
     —I Kings 18:24

July 4, Thompson, Ohio

Under threat of drizzle after a long drought,
rides the oldest fire chief in the nation
on board an antique fire wagon pulled by horses
around the dried-up lawn of the square,
past his firehouse,
past the sausage stand, past the children
holding plastic bags, waiting
for their sweet reward for being young,
the storm of candy.
Then, his wife on a trailer,
waving—not *hand, hand, wrist, wrist,*
elbow, elbow, beauty queen manner—
but slicing at the air
as though counting down a knockout.
Then the bawling band and the color guard
of veterans with poles protruding
from their special crotch-level flag-holding belts,
and the Harley bikers in leather husks,
and the ladies walking beribboned pugs,
which snap their vestigial jaws.
Then the feed store owner throwing
samples of dog food
to the children clutching plastic bags.
Then the Vacation Bible School float—
a hospital theme this year,
one boy in scrubs leaning over
another lying under a blanket
on a folding table gurney, squirming

as the truck jolts its tow.
And finally, a chubby girl
in an iconic blue gingham dress,
hair in braids, red shoes,
leading a light brown cow
with a tin funnel on its head
and sheets of
aluminum foil
duct-taped to its body,
over its sides and flanks,
steely tape reaching under its tail;
somewhere inside, a heart beats.
No sun breaks through, nor any rain.

THE FIG

There's a wasp inside each fig—this
sounds like a parable but isn't. The fig
needs its specific wasp to pollinate, to ripen.
The flowers of the fig lie hidden within.

This sounds like a parable, but isn't. The female
wasp crawls inside, a tunnel not wide enough for wings,
which shed. And trapped, she hides her eggs in flowers
which turn to galls instead of seeds, and then to wasps.

Blind males emerge first and find females, still in galls, not
    hatched,
and gnaw a hole through to mate, then, doomed, dig tunnels
only females follow to leave the fig, whose flesh is flower.
Then females, now wasps, pollen-flecked, fly off to visit other
    figs.

The fig I chew is female; male flowers bear only mated wasps
    and pollen,
and wasps can only reproduce in males. But wasps still enter
female figs, spread the pollen from the males, then have no place
to lay their eggs. The fig in my mouth is female, and inside,
    likely,

a wasp, who died confused, wondering what went wrong,
what strange flowers she'd found and didn't need.
But there, too, crushed by teeth, the seeds of figs, the true fruits,
that now won't grow to trees. This sounds like a love story,

but isn't. The fig eats the female wasps, the blind males, the
galls that fail to hatch. Each dissolves, unnoticed on my

tongue—an unsolved murder; a fairy tale; a parable of sweet flowers, a flightless secret, a nourishing grave.

HOMAGE TO SMALL HURTS

The euphoria of climb hangs upon
risk, so where have you gone, playgrounds
of steel, of sound concrete,
                          obstinate—

a lesson, yes, I needed to learn? You allowed us all
to break our bones, to see beneath our blank
skin—
        persecuted knees, ephemeral teeth, the sanguine world

of gravity—the school of let go
and fall. We scrambled up geodesic hemispheres,
hooked our legs, dropped;
                          we burned

down molten slides and hopped off swings into brief,
soft air above sure ground—smack and
crumble—
        we knew this would happen. Then

on to the merry-go-round—waiting to tumble,
dizzy, the binge of spin—
I have to stop going in circles.
                          Even our words

spiraled—grandiloquent insults, rudderless,
brags and bets, the jeopardy of lies.

                          Children
of today, with your liabilities, your plastic
structures, uncalamitous tubes, bark dust—
                          I worry.

This is play—

        learn to walk away, weaving;
leave the rest to rust.

FRAMING THE SHOT

(after Graciela Iturbide's El Gallo, Juchitán,
Oaxaca, Mexico, 1986*)*

Light takes a crooked path
through lens, then mirror, then ground glass, then prism.
When it gets to you, the world has been cropped
into a frame,
                    an amputated view
carved from its surroundings.
                          A boy
backs against a wall, his black hair
tufted, as he holds to his cheeks
the white wings
of a rooster, flight
feathers spreading from his temples
like a mask. The bird
is dead,
comb flopped over, neck slung down. Skin
shows through the feathers on the belly. Sharp claws
hang from shanks.
                   Somewhere there is the woman
with her hands on its throat.
                       Somewhere, the rooster—
crowing that morning in the scratched yard,
pulling its whole body up before the beak
blasts open, the chest wheezing
like a siren running down.
                  Somewhere,
the carcass—on the table in pieces,
the onion chopped neatly into teeth.
                     But here against
the wall, the boy presses the bird's back
to his lips.

HISTORICAL MARKER
PARTIALLY OBSCURED BY SHRUBS

to support the Union
matrons, sanitary agents
role in promoting
sick
moved with her family to
She married
became governor
drowned
wounded at the Battle
thereupon dedicated herself
improper sanitation
met Abraham Lincoln
hospitals
United States Army
closed in 1874.

Loneliness as a Tour of Covered Bridges, Ashtabula County, Ohio

Single lane, only one vehicle can pass through at a time. Still, I never have to wait.

Covered bridges only remain on roads no one uses.

Hand-painted sign at a farm: Sorry no grapes this year crops froze do not know where else to buy grapes...

In fields, in front of unpainted barns, in gravel driveways—tractors, temporarily or permanently still, the dominant population.

Bridge on pilings over nothing but grass, the creek fifty feet away. A hundred years ago it washed downstream and someone brought it back.

Trailers capsized in waist-high weeds, goldenrod, and teasel. Trailers veiled behind saplings. Windows dark, the haze of inoccupation.

Trailers in mown yards, foil insulation board tacked around the bottom. Trailers with clotheslines of pants. Trailer with a blue inflatable shark lying in the grass, slowly letting out someone's breath.

An uncovered wooden bridge lasts only a few years.

This sign, again and again, on the side of the road, posted to mailboxes, on stakes in ditches, a communal intention, a code, a prayer: fresh brown eggs $1.50.

My truck engine's rattle held in by walls, roof, suggesting another machine's presence, a follower.

The maw of wood, laminated arch, trusses.

Road missing. I compare map to my perceptions, find no correlation, scan land empty of reference.

Ghost of passage, bridge lost to arson. Someone piled tires inside, lit them on fire.

Signs at small cemeteries, their headstones fainting: closed at dusk.

On one end of bridge, sign for lost dog, $1000 reward. On the other end, sign for different lost dog, no reward.

Ingress and egress, what makes a tunnel.

Dead end at missing bridge overlooking woods. No evidence of the story of a runaway truck, of the hazards of impact.

The gas gauge lingers near empty. I consider my course, my miscalculations.

Vacant house, unlit pyre of furnishings in drive, tubes of metal chair legs, blaze of upholstery.

Bridge in my mind, far away, where a boy once took me. I recognize the bridge in moonlight, water moving below iced-over falls. But which boy? How did we get there?

Bridges gone one hundred years recalled, though no one alive ever saw them.

Lazy river of drought. Things still move on.

Warning. Private. No trespassing. To trespass is to disrupt the absence of you.

SKY DIVE

On a road I take
back to where I belong
when I forget where I'm going,
make the wrong turn,
                    a man slammed into land,
dropped
from the sky of a mostly clear day
at the exact moment
                  I considered,
in my garden,
the ground—its softness—
while planting seeds—
the lightest in my palm
picked up by wind, shunning the rows.

Someone came across the misplaced body,
near the spot where two days before, in my car,
with its tires perpetually rolling, I'd passed
                       a boy—
wearing straw hat, blue pants, suspenders—
riding bareback on a white and soil-colored pony,
his hand swatting its flank—
jockey in an inconclusive race.

Once a man rode a balloon into
the stratosphere,
where the stars are more starry, and
                  stepped out,
in a pressurized suit,
to fall for a while, closing in on sound,
but not catching it. He said
he had no sense

of how fast he moved along the path
$$of down$$
before he pulled the chute over him
like a cloud;
          later he held
a pencil, did the math.

Terminal velocity
is the speed at which acceleration
no longer matters.
               It happens when

all that can touch a body
               has.
When over the turned fields,
the speckles of roofs, the faint roads,
you pull a cord

and your bright chute
fails to send you anywhere.

SKYWAY DRIVE-IN THEATER, MADISON, OHIO

The term is "dark," not closed, as though
this white screen looming through locust, sumac,
merely abides, suspended above
the tree-penetrated parking lot. Today's feature:
only faint shadows in sun—
film blanc. Gone, the *new In-A-Car speakers.*
Adjust volume to suit yourself.
Instead, inescapable soundtrack: the Doppler
traffic of Highway 20, crescendo, fade,
crescendo—this familiar story. Girl trespasses
scratching for clues, finds
abandoned ruins. The projection building
and concession stand, now a concrete slab
among wild strawberry, yarrow, goldenrod.
I'm the audience for this plot
of land. Once, there was *no need to leave your car*
at any time. Because climbing out is how you
get in trouble—the weeds wrap around you,
dogs snarl off screen, sirens whine by.
Across the road, someone's cut down the woods
to make a vacant lot.
No place can disappear.
2 shows nightly rain or clear.
The first, romance and adventure:
a storm passes through, men unite,
a hero swoops in to save the little town.
The second, futuristic epic:
dot of girl alone in brushy field,
strange monolith crumbling, a star-studded
glimpse of the end of the world.

64

MISSING

A man went missing
just up the road; they know exactly where
his whereabouts became unknown—a witnessed
vanishing, like rapture.
His car rolled over,
then slid a hundred yards into the parking lot of
God's Tabernacle, a prefab church with
undetectable parish,
across from
the more congregational
tavern promising spirits and thirty-cent wings.
Speed
played a factor, and probably alcohol,
and, indirectly, drugs.
My son is no angel, says his father,
but he is a good kid.
A bystander testified
the man walked away from the crash,
leaving
some woman unconscious in the passenger seat,
leaving
behind two children at home,
parole, alleged involvement in local
meth lab, past associates eager to
assault him,
as they had weeks before—
his leg in a cast as he limped into January
turning to February turning to four years,
fading precisely.
I didn't know the guy,
though maybe I've seen him,
or his

absence, or really, the hole
he fell down,
            but when
you're running past a grey snake, you don't
stop to check if it's
a rope.

Measuring Exposure

(after Nina Berman's Wounded U.S. Marine Returns
Home From Iraq to Marry, *2006)*

Your light meter believes
that the shadows
        and highlights
and tones in between
average out to eighteen-percent gray, a shade like
the hide of something tough.

                So, the young bride's
white sleeveless gown
cancels out the groom's midnight blue dress uniform.
But how much light do we find
in her red bouquet of roses
with its one white flower?
             Or the portrait studio's
all-purpose backdrop?
          Or the reflection off his
bald head, his facial features lost to scars, ear fused
into jaw, nose into mouth? Inside, a plastic dome
has replaced his shattered skull. His left hand,
a prosthetic, deflated of gesture.
His expression, entombed;
              and hers,
a blank neutrality
we ache to shape into something—
                shock,
sadness, the bravery of vows.
           Yet moments earlier
she was smiling,
        or maybe moments later.

One flash defined
the suicide bomber,
blacked out everything before.

The couple
in the photo become famous, their story
detached from them, given its own
lasting future, an icon
to adopt.

But it's a wedding photo,
a posed instant before a life,
in which
he takes pills to smooth out
several shapes of pain,
to make possible a day's routine. In a year,
they divorce.
Still, always doubt a little
that bright and dark add up to gray.

CLOTHESLINE

for Mary Henninge (1935-2015)

Mine, anchored on one end by a single wooden post set near a field of milkweed, nylon cord stretched to the tall fence enclosing the chicken yard. Hardly technology, this modest appliance, and yet I love it more than my ice maker, always coughing out another cube. My mind hangs there, with the wincing underwear, the bra's breasts of breeze. Beyond the milkweed, killdeer circle and keen, drag their unbroken wings, luring someone away from their eggs. *I'm hurt, I'm hurt, so follow me.* I used to chatter with my rooster and his murmuring hens as I clipped up towels. But some dog got in the chicken yard days ago, snapped necks; silence from behind the fence now, and feathers. Even wrung, the washed bear damp weight until they shed it in the wind. The shirts trapeze, sleeves reaching. The dress, without my stiff waist, finally graceful. And how it all clamps on—the pin's beak of wooden shims, eye of spiraled wire, grooves to bite and hold. The planet's riffling lung. The sun. The invisible work of the line—that fundamental road through space. The simplest path between two points, between what needs doing and what's been done.

FIRST PLACE AT THE COUNTY FAIR

The Children

The children want their hands in full pockets,
    their hands around sticks of sweetness,
                        of grease and salt.
The stomach only needs;
        the mouth tastes and wants. The mouth says
    corndog, chilidog, steak sandwich, barbeque,
    funnel cake, onion ring, elephant ear, french fry,
    fried dough.

The children want what they can't finish.

The Carnies

The carnies don't want the young girls.
They want the young girls to think they want
                     the young girls and
    be afraid and want
          to be afraid because fear leads to
    want of soft toys.
The carnies want the soft toys to go away,
    bears and cats, dogs and monkeys, hanging, feeble with
    loneliness,
        loneliness overpowering any cute,
    like the young girls,
            their wanting.

The Swine

The swine wants to stop being smacked with the stick
    by the boy leading her around the ring with
    the other swine being smacked with sticks,
                              on the neck,
    on the flank.
The boy wants the blue ribbon finally this year, but
the swine wants to return to the old stall of hay, but
        the boy swats her rump with a flat hand,
    showing long sides, good muscle, a fine ham.
The swine wants to be called Pig, not swine.

The Chicken Flying Contest

The chicken would maybe like to fly, but
now she wants small hands,
            her name whispered,
                    her feathers
    caressed and straightened.
She wants to please,
        to lay the egg warm in her box.
Flight—
    too much today, with the sun high,
        the grandstands' laughter,
    her cries—she is lobbed
            into the sky, her wings,
disappointed.

The Grange

The American Legion knows their pancakes sell better than
the Grange's pancakes, each stack fortified
with two sausages.

The Judge

The judge wants a glass of water to wear down the feel
    of baked goods, each cake giving moistly under fork—
        his tongue numb with crumbs and icing,
        his teeth sweet with polite smiles—
                      the ladies
    with their necks—
              What does he know, anyway?
Each loaf has touched a lady's hand,
          has risen.

The Politician

The politician wants the people in their shorts to see
                   his tie,
    his buttoned throat, his slacks, his polished
                shoes, like
    speeches, stepping gingerly
          through the barns.

The Cow

The cow prides herself on lowing, her udders full
                to show what
    she will give.
The sign tells her pedigree, her dam and sire, her age—
              but she is
    ageless, a title passing
        on and on, a ritual of tug and milk.

She wants to go to the field where she will
    follow the cow following
        the cow following the cow,

their trail,
                    indelible and dusty.

The Amish

The Amish walk among us, like props.

The Draft Horse

The woman brushes the draft horse, the scent of oil and leather,
and he wants her to stop so he can
                              pull the cart, his black yoke
           tempting
                    his neck—something to resist,
           to push—he hears
                         the wheels turn, the sound of
           surrender—
                    he submits to
                              the brush, to sensation,
           lifts his hooves
                         into her small hand for her
to check his shoes.

The Young Men

The young men want the carnies
                              to want the girls,
                                        so they can aim
           darts at balloons, throw balls,
                              ride the mechanical bull
                    of the girls' attentions—
                                   one hand flapping,
           bodies bucking;

73

they feel the programmed whir and turn,
            the intoxicating toss.
The girls, cute,
            dragging soft toys.

The Manure Man

The man with the wheelbarrow of manure wants everything
to stop
            moving for awhile,
                        so he can catch up on his scooping,
            each barn a distinct stink,
                        the animals' particular filth,
            the coops and stalls and cages.
                        He sees it is all
unclean, all appetite.

The Children

The children want dubious whirling contrivances
                                    lifting them.
They want the amusement of gears and belts,
                        shuddering cars,
            safety bars straining—
they want to see a sane world through
                        giddiness, their faces
            to wax and wane through revolutions;
to think
            I could die of course. I could step outside
                        this cage—

            the ride burning out its
                        frenzy,
bringing them around.

Acknowledgements

Thank you to Russian photographer Maria Ionova-Gribina for use of the cover photo. Ionova-Gribina studied photography in Moscow, where she was born and raised. Her work is in private collections in both Russia and elsewhere and has appeared in numerous exhibitions at galleries and museums, including the Moscow Museum of Modern Art. This photo belongs to her series *Natura Morta*. See more of her work at www.ionovagribina.ru.

The following poems appeared in these journals:

"Egg": *32 Poems*

"Phobia Poems," "How to Use a Single-lens Reflex," "Adjusting the Depth of Field": *AGNI* online journal

"Magic Fingers," "Workbench": *Barnwood*

"First Place at the County Fair": *Black Warrior Review*

"Stinging Things": *The Boiler Journal*

"Cow Puppet": *The Cincinnati Review*

"Love Poem with Bodies": *Cold Mountain Review*

"Amish Boy with Remote Control Car": *Crab Orchard Review*

"Skyway Drive-In Theater, Madison, Ohio": *Devil's Lake*

"Missing": *Free State Review*

"To Bear": *Hayden's Ferry Review*

"Killing Songbirds the Compassionate Way": *Meridian*

"Mole," "Sky Dive," and "From Old Dr. Carlin's Receipt Book and Household Physician": *Mid-American Review*

"The Middle School Cheerleader," "Amish Boy Gesturing at the Road," "Measuring Exposure": *Moon City Review*

"Clothesline": *A Narrow Fellow*

"Daffodils": *Notre Dame Review*

"Homage to Small Hurts," "Historical Marker Partially Obscured by Shrubs," "Historical Marker, Rest Stop, Jackson County, Wisconsin," and "Rickey Henderson Breaks the Record for Stolen Bases in a Season, Milwaukee, 1982": *Smartish Pace*

"Birthday Party Magician": *Swink*

"Bluing": *Sycamore Review*

"The Sacrifice" (as "July 4, Thompson, Ohio"): *Wake: Great Lakes Thought and Culture*

"Rickey Henderson Breaks the Record for Stolen Bases in a Season, Milwaukee, 1982" appears in the anthology *New Poetry from the Midwest 2014* (New American Press)

Many thanks to Ohio Arts Council for support through Individual Excellence Awards in 2006, 2010, and 2014.

Ohio Arts Council

ABOUT GOLD WAKE PRESS

Gold Wake Press, an independent publisher, was founded in Boston, Massachusetts in 2008 by J. Michael Wahlgren. All in-print Gold Wake titles are available at Amazon, barnesandnoble.com, and via order from your local bookstore.

Adam Crittenden's *Blood Eagle*

Joshua Butts' *New to the Lost Coast*

Mary Buchinger Bodwell's *Aerialist*

Becca J. R. Lachman's *Other Acreage*

Lesley Jenike's *Holy Island*

Tasha Cotter's *Some Churches*

Nick Courtright's *Let There Be Light*

Kyle McCord's *You Are Indeed an Elk, But This is Not the Forest You Were Born to Graze*

Hannah Stephenson's *In the Kettle, the Shriek*

Kathleen Rooney's *Robinson Alone*

About the author

Poet and essayist Mary Quade's collection *Guide to Native Beasts* won the 2003 Cleveland State University Poetry Center First Book Prize. Her work has been awarded an Oregon Literary Fellowship and three Ohio Arts Council Individual Excellence Awards. Her poems appear in anthologies, including *On the Wing: American Poems of Air and Space Flight* (University of Iowa); *New Voices: Contemporary Poetry from the United States* (Irish Pages); and *New Poetry from the Midwest 2014* (New American Press). She is an associate professor of English at Hiram College in Ohio, where she teaches creative writing.

CPSIA information can be obtained
at www.ICGtesting.com
Printed in the USA
FFHW021554210219
50611493-55980FF

9 781944 788186